SINGLE PARENTS

The Essential Guide

Need
— 2 —
Know

Sarah
Edwards

First published in Great Britain in 2008 by
Need2Know
Remus House
Coltsfoot Drive
Peterborough
PE2 9JX
Telephone 01733 898103
Fax 01733 313524
www.need2knowbooks.co.uk

Need2Know is an imprint of Forward Press Ltd.
www.forwardpress.co.uk
All Rights Reserved
© Sarah Edwards 2008
SB ISBN 978-1-86144-055-6
Cover photograph: Jupiter Images

Contents

Introduction

Becoming a single parent can be a huge shock. You may well find that your life becomes an emotional roller coaster. You will feel strong and capable one day and completely hopeless and scared the next.

You will feel exhausted, angry, sad, lonely and helpless - often all in the same 24 hour period - but these feelings will change and you will be able to find a way through the rough times. I hope that this book will give you some ideas for dealing with the difficult early days of single parenting.

Whether you made the decision to bring up your children alone, or if your partner has left the family home, you will face the same challenges and dilemmas on a daily basis. However, everyone's situation is different, and it is important to remember that you are not alone - even though you may feel isolated, lonely and sad.

Last year in the UK there were 141,750 divorces and 138,332 children under the age of 16 had parents who went through a divorce. Nearly two thirds of those children were under 11 years old (source: www.divorceonline.co.uk).

Not all single parent families exist as a result of divorce. Thousands of couples who are not married but have children together, split up every year. In many other cases, a parent has died. One quarter of all children in the UK live in one-parent families and nine out of 10 single-parent homes are headed by women.

This book has been written by an experienced single parent to try and give you inspiration, advice and encouragement as you start your new life with your children.

Becoming a single parent is an emotional time, but you will need to consider the practicalities of your new life as well. From accepting your new situation and managing your home to working, looking after yourself, dating again and establishing new relationships - there are many aspects of your life that will need attention.

Many parents overlook their own needs because they are so busy concentrating on their children. This book helps you achieve balance in your life and tries to offer solutions that will make your life easier, happier and less stressful. It is important to build time into your week that doesn't just involve household chores, school runs and work. You should give yourself time to think and plan for your family's future - and have some fun and relaxation as well.

'Many parents overlook their own needs because they are so busy concentrating on their children. This book helps you achieve balance in your life and tries to offer solutions that will make your life easier, happier and less stressful.'

I have asked single parents who have successfully started their lives again to share their stories with you to demonstrate what can be achieved over time. One of the most important things to remember is that your situation will not be the same as anyone else's, so do not be tempted to put yourself under pressure to do too much too soon. This is particularly true if you have very young children.

It is all too easy to pick up a magazine and read stories of parents who are running businesses and living what would appear to be an enviable lifestyle. In reality, these people will not be facing the same challenges as you on a daily basis and trying to aspire to their lifestyle will only add to your stress levels.

It's much better to accept your situation and move forward slowly at your own pace so that you can stay in control. Planning is an important part of the process when you suddenly find yourself on your own with your children and throughout the book I will give you tips and advice to try and help you get organised.

From getting a family diary to creating a planner for the kitchen wall and getting in control of your finances, there are lots of simple ways to get your life back on track and make improvements. The ideas that I have written about have all been tried and tested by single parents and their children, so I know they work!

The very fact that you have picked up this book is a positive step in the right direction. I cannot promise miracles and your life will never be the same again, but in time you will find that you will start to rebuild your life. The challenges and problems that you faced early on will get easier!

There is a lot of help, support and advice available for single parents, particularly on the Internet through new chat rooms, support groups and even dating websites just for single parents. At the back of the book you will find a list of some of the best and newest resources available to help single parents just like you.

Good luck and best wishes.

Chapter One

On My Own

You may be reading this book because your partner has just left you, because your partner has died or because you have decided to leave your partner. Whatever the reason for becoming a single parent, you will experience a multitude of emotions and it is important to remember that this is normal.

Acceptance is the first stage of moving forward and in this first chapter we will look at ways you can help yourself to accept your situation and plan your life.

Obviously your life is going to have to change and adapt to meet your new situation as you will now find yourself responsible for every aspect of running your home and caring for your children.

You will need to plan your days and weeks differently from now on and make time to deal with all the tasks that were previously dealt with by your partner. Single parenting is incredibly tiring and it is not just about taking care of the children. Bills still have to be paid; you still need to put food on the table every night and your home and car will still need to be taken care of. If you are working, you may need to either take some time off or work part time - all this requires planning and only comes when you accept your new situation.

Acceptance

Now is the time to begin to accept your situation and the way it makes you feel, and to try and start planning and organising your time as effectively as possible. It is possible that circumstances beyond your control decided how your life would be from now on, which makes being a single parent even harder to deal with. Even if you made the decision to bring up your children alone, you will still encounter difficulties.

Finding yourself alone with the huge task of bringing up your children is a shock. Everyone's situation is different and if your partner has died you will have different emotions to deal with. There are some excellent support groups and networks available who offer help and advice to both parents and children. Some contact information for these specialist agencies can be found in the help list at the back of this book. You may find that although the thought of talking to a complete stranger is daunting at first, professional help may well be one of your first stepping stones.

Taking the decision to leave your partner is rarely done lightly. You may have left because you found yourself in an abusive or damaging relationship that made you fear for the safety of yourself and your children. If this is the case you have probably already accepted that you will be bringing your children up alone, but you will still need support. You will need to sort out somewhere to live, find out about benefits and working and make decisions about giving your partner access to see his or her children.

If your partner has left you and it wasn't planned, you will no doubt feel angry, sad, resentful and scared - often all at the same time. Your emotions can change on a regular basis and one day you might feel as though you can deal with anything, while on another you may feel at a complete loss and be unable to cope with the simplest tasks.

- Accept that your situation will be different to that of other single parents.

- You will experience lots of different emotions and this is normal. Explain to people what has happened and that you will have good days and bad days - they will understand.

- Seek professional help (see help list at the back of the book for a list of useful contacts). Counsellors are experts at helping people just like you and they understand how you are feeling.

- In the early days of single parenting remember that completing the smallest task is really important. Make sure you have realistic expectations of what you know you can cope with on a daily basis and don't over stretch yourself.

- It is a cliché, but take one day at a time. Your life will never be the same again. Although it may seem impossible to believe it at the moment, things will get better and you will find your way.

Dealing with emotions

Becoming a single parent is an emotional roller coaster. Bereavement alone is incredibly difficult to handle, particularly when children are involved, but you will inevitably feel a sense of loss whatever your circumstances.

Being left is frightening and sad; it makes you angry and can fill you with resentment and mistrust. It is important to recognise these feelings and accept that how you feel is to be expected. People who are close to you will learn to understand and accept that you are going through a traumatic time and they won't expect you to put on a brave face, so don't put yourself under pressure to suppress your emotions. They have to come out at some point and it's best to do that now rather than bottle it all up for later.

Facing our fears is how we move our lives forward, so although you may think that being in denial may help you in the short term because it distracts you from your problems, in the long term these feelings will come back to haunt you. It is hard, but try to face your feelings and work through them. Being open and honest with your children about how you are feeling is important too and professional counsellors can help you find a strategy to manage your emotions and protect your children at the same time.

- Don't deny how you are feeling. It is much healthier to be honest with yourself and others. If people understand why you are behaving in a certain way they can help you.

- Expect to be surprised by your emotions. One day you may be able to cope with life and the next you may feel overwhelmed.

- Make things as achievable as possible. If you are really struggling to cope, ask for help and take a step back.

- Your children are your priority, so accepting your emotions will help them in the long run as well as you. Being able to talk honestly with them about why you are sad or worried can help, but be careful not to worry them with things that they really can't do anything about.

- Seek professional help, starting with your GP or health visitor. It's not a sign of weakness and it doesn't mean you are losing you mind - it just means that you need someone to look at your situation in a different way and guide you through the emotional maze you are in.

'When I was first on my own with my two children I was mortified. I was the only person in my family and my social group who had been left by their husband - I was embarrassed.'

Telling people what has happened

Being a single parent is not unusual; in every class in every school you will find a high percentage of children who, for a variety of reasons, are in one-parent families.

Feeling sensitive and awkward about your situation is perfectly natural, but you will start to feel more positive if you tell people what has happened and why. If you don't want to go into lots of detail then that's fine and there is no reason why you should. In time you will find it easier to talk about things and you may even find that talking about what has happened really helps.

Be assured that people probably will talk about you, but your close friends and family will do this because they are worried and want to help you. It is difficult not to be defensive and assume that you are the subject of the latest gossip, but try really hard not to get upset by this. Your focus should be you and your children and finding the best way to communicate your situation to the people in your life who really matter.

> 'I remember pushing my baby in his pram through town for the first time and not wearing a wedding ring. I was sure that everyone could see I wasn't married and were judging me. I wanted to shout that he had left me and it wasn't my fault.'

- There is no need to make a public announcement about your new status, just tell the people who really need to know and who you want to know.

- It does help to talk, so gather people around you who you really trust. If they are your friends they will listen.

- You will feel better when people know what has happened, so be brave and take the plunge.

- You will probably find it much easier to tell people without your children being around. Try to find a quiet time to make phone calls, send texts or emails, or to meet your friends and family face to face.

- Once you have told people they will inevitably want to contact you regularly to make sure you are alright. Although their intentions are admirable, this can also be stressful. Either screen your calls or politely say that you will call them if you need them and that right now you just need some time alone with your children. You can always make some time when the children are in bed to call people back.

Getting organised

Accepting your situation and the realisation that you are now a single parent is the first stage of moving your life forward. There is no way of knowing how long this will take you as everyone is different. However, life does go on and things still have to happen, so being organised is an important part of the process.

There are various people who will need to know about your change in circumstances. The first step in dealing with this is to make a checklist of people and organisations that you will need to contact (see below).
These contacts may not apply to everyone and are given as an example. You can add your own and prioritise them according to your own individual needs.

Checklist

Organisation	Contact name	Contact number	Outcome
Bank			
Doctor			
Schools			
Local Authority			
Employer			

'Making lists and trying to be organised on top of all the stress and heartbreak I was going through felt like a chore to be honest and there were times when I almost resented having to spend time doing it! However, it really helped me get back on track and take control. All of a sudden things were actually starting to happen. Now I keep an action list with me and tick things off when I have done them. It's a good feeling to be back in control!' Susie, 26, single mum to two girls.

- Create your checklist and start working through it. Keep a note of who you have spoken to.

- Allocate some time to letter writing - some people will need you to actually provide written proof of your change of circumstances.

- Keep your expectations realistic; use a tick list of daily tasks so you know what has to happen.

- Answer the phone and open your mail - don't be afraid of facing things. There will always be someone who you can call on for help.

- Try to keep on top of essential tasks like paying bills and insuring the car.

Daily routine

Planning and being organised might seem like an enormous task because of all the extra things that you will now have to factor into your day. It is possible that you won't have been responsible for doing the weekly shop, servicing the car or paying all the bills before and that these jobs were all shared between the two of you.

It will now be up to you to organise the school run, make sure that PE kits and packed lunches are organised and dental appointments are kept. You will also have to think about things such as attending school events and helping with homework, as well as making sure the bills are paid.

One of the simplest ways to keep on top of your daily and weekly routines is to have a family planner. A big diary is fine, but you may find that a wall planner, blackboard or a big piece of paper stuck to a kitchen cupboard door works best for you.

As well as entering daily events and appointments, a planner can be used to make a note of chores and jobs that have to happen in the home - even the youngest child can help with some of these.

- Being organised sounds like a chore in itself, but it is a good part of a management strategy, so find one that works for you and stick to it.

- Make sure that everyone in the family understands why being organised is important and that it will make everyone's life easier.

- Make some time each day and week to plan ahead. Put as much as you can on the planner and then tick off tasks as they are completed.

- Get ahead with school runs and organise a lift share with other parents in your area or offer to walk each other's children to school. If you are a working parent, organisation really is key. Wash and iron school uniforms in advance if possible so that you don't have a last minute panic.

- Being organised and planning ahead will help you deal with every aspect of your new life. If you have a clear idea of what you have to achieve, chances are that you will, and you will begin to feel positive about things. If you wander aimlessly through your life without any focus you will become frustrated at your lack of achievement.

Summing Up

Accepting your new situation will be the hardest thing that you have to do. Everyone deals with it differently and you will feel alone and abandoned as well as angry, frustrated and sad.

Having complete responsibility for yourself and your children is frightening and fraught with potential pitfalls; you can find a way through it because every year millions of us do!

Remember that although you may feel alone, you are not on your own; friends and family will want to support you, so let them. Don't try and do everything yourself and be realistic about what you can achieve.

Be honest with yourself about how you feel because once you acknowledge the difficulties you are facing, you will be able to find the right way to manage your emotions and plan how you are going to live your life from now on.

You are at the beginning of a new journey and there will be bumps in the road, but ultimately you will find your way.

Chapter Two

Children

You may have always been a single parent and knew that even before your baby was born that you would be bringing them up alone, or you may be newly single and struggling to cope with the demands that parenting places on you. This chapter helps to guide you through the process of communicating with your children about your situation.

Parents tend to think that younger children are not able to understand adult emotions, but this is not necessarily true. Your children know when something in the home is wrong, even if they can't verbally express to you what the problem is. The best way to answer any questions your children may have is honestly. You can tailor your answers based on your children's age, but be aware that keeping important information from your children may not necessarily be a good idea.

Talk to them

The best thing you can do to help your children deal with divorce or splitting up is to let them talk. After you've explained your decision, make sure that you let your children know that they can talk to you about their feelings. If they know they can always come to you to tell you how the divorce is affecting them, they are less likely to be angry with you and less likely to let the divorce affect other things in their lives, such as school activities or relationships with friends.

Children tend to feel unwanted or unloved when their parents are splitting up; they often blame themselves and feel that something they have done has caused their parents to separate. It's important that you let your children know that they are still loved very much by both parents and that this is not their fault. Your children still need to know that they are part of a family and that both parents are making an effort to be an active part of their lives. You should also make sure that your children are not being forced to choose one parent over another. This can be difficult sometimes, since one parent usually has primary custody.

See *Divorce and Separation – The Essential Guide* for further information on talking to your children.

Checklist

- Be honest and open with your children.

- Don't overload them or over share your emotions and feelings with them, as this is a huge responsibility for children to have to deal with.

- If there is an absent parent, try to keep on good terms - if only for the sake of your children.

- If you are tired and stressed, tell your children but don't get angry. Just explain that you have a lot to do and need a bit of help from them.

'It's important that you let your children know that they are still loved very much by both parents and that this is not their fault.'

Routine

Routine is key for single-parent families. There is a lot to do and most of it will fall on your shoulders; if you don't have a system in place you will fall at the first hurdle!

Everyone can benefit from having a simple domestic routine to stick to and children respond particularly well to this. Quite apart from the fact that a routine is important to make sure everything gets done, routine can be a huge comfort to children, especially if their parents have recently split up.

Simple things like having a family planner stuck to the kitchen cupboard door with a list of everything that has to happen each day is a great way to keep on top of things. If you can stick to regular meal times and bed times as well then you will find life becomes a lot less stressful. During the school or working week, try really hard to stick to a routine that means homework gets done, school uniforms are washed and ironed and everyone gets to bed at a reasonable time. Then at the weekends you can afford to relax the rules a bit.

- A routine is helpful for everyone in a busy house - especially for children.

- Make a simple family planner with days of the week and tasks clearly marked on it. Involve the whole family in the process and then they are more likely to remember things!

- Rewards are good! Children can be praised and rewarded for helping around the house with small tasks that will make a big difference to a single parent's workload. Keep a reward chart marked with stars or smiley faces and then at the end of each week add up all the stars and give your children a small treat.

- Be firm with friends! If you want dinner on the table at 6pm so your children are bathed and in bed by 7.30pm, make sure everyone knows that you will be busy at those times.

- If your children take part in regular activities, try really hard to keep them in the routine of going to their classes or groups. It's important that children have structure in place and do things regularly that they enjoy.

School

If you are a new single parent and your children attend a school, nursery, playgroup or preschool, it is a good idea to let teachers know as soon as possible. This way, they can keep an eye on your children's behaviour and will be able to make allowances for any changes in the way they act when they are away from you.

You will also find that teachers, nursery managers and play leaders are all trained to understand how difficult things can be for children from single-parent families and they will be sympathetic and supportive of the whole family. They will also have access to support and advice that you may not be aware of, which can be beneficial to your situation.

- Try to attend as many school events as possible. It's really important for your children to be supported in this way and to see that you want to see them take part in events with their friends and fellow pupils.

- Keep talking to the teachers. If your children have a home/school diary and you have had a particularly stressful weekend then put a note in the book to let the teacher know what has happened.

- School is part of your routine, so to keep mornings as stress-free as possible get organised the night before. This way, if you do have a child who is reluctant to go to school, you will have time and space to stay calm rather than rushing and getting stressed.

- Get to know other parents at the school gate. Not everyone is sociable and if you are a newly single parent you may not want to broadcast this to all and sundry. However, you can guarantee that there will be a lot more people in your situation than you might think - you may even make some new friends.

- Don't be coerced into sitting on committees, fundraising groups or becoming a school governor unless you really have the time to do it. Single parents who work part time around the children are often targeted by committees to take part in fundraising events and other school projects, but we are the parents with the least time available so think very carefully before you commit to anything!

The absent parent

Children have a right to see both of their parents - if they want to - and it is important to remember this and do everything you can to try and help them as much as possible. This may not be an easy task for you, particularly if you do not get on well with your ex. However, it is important to remember that whatever the reasons are for you becoming a single parent, children cannot be blamed and must be allowed to see both parents.

Obviously, in some cases it may not be possible, safe or sensible for your children to see the absent parent. In these cases you will need to take detailed advice from professionals who can help you.

If you have a regular access arrangement this will help as you can include visits or overnight stays with the absent parent as part of your family routine and add all the details to the planner. If you can stick to the same days/times each week or month then you will all benefit as you can plan other activities around the times that the children are with their other parent.

As well as giving your children valuable time with their other parent, you also need to think about your need for space and a bit of time off as well. It is very easy to forget ourselves and to feel guilty for wanting any time away from our children, but we are better parents and nicer people to be around if we can all get some time off occasionally!

Tips for an easier life

- If you don't have regular access arrangements with the absent parent then consider putting them in place.

- If the relationship with the absent parent has been difficult historically, you may need to attend mediation or seek other professional advice.

- Put your children's needs first. If they want to see their other parent then do everything you can to make it happen. If they are not keen then discuss this with them and try and find a solution.

- Don't feel guilty for having some time off from parenting. We all need a break and you are not abandoning your children by having a few hours to yourself each week.

- Listen to your children. You may find that they behave differently after visiting the absent parent and you will need to find out why. Instead of interrogating them the minute they walk through the door, let them come to you, because they will!

The health and wellbeing of your children

This has to be paramount and is something we are doing all the time without even realising it! If your children are getting plenty of sleep, eating well and enjoying an active lifestyle with plenty of fresh air and socialising opportunities - you are doing a good job!

Routine once again plays a big part in the overall wellbeing and health of all children, as it is important to make time for being together as a family and have regular meal times and bed times.

'As well as giving your children valuable time with their parent, you also need to think about your need for space and a bit of time off as well.'

Life will be hectic in a single-parent household and it is easy to let things slide. Before you know it, bedtime has been pushed back an hour because supper was late as you spent an hour on the phone chatting! Of course you must have time for yourself as well, but for a household to be happy and healthy, meal times and bed times have to become almost sacred!

Tired children are grumpy, lethargic and uncommunicative. They also argue with their siblings and are more prone to becoming run down and catching every illness that is currently doing the rounds at school.

To try and keep things well balanced and harmonious, insist that you all eat a healthy supper together every evening, go to bed at a reasonable time and get plenty of fresh air. Children perform better at school if they are well rested and in good health, and you will be a better parent if you follow the same rules.

- A healthy, well balanced diet is a great start for a child's health and wellbeing.

- Health professionals such as your GP or health visitor will always be happy to give you advice if you are worried about your children.

- Early nights and lots of fresh air and activity are the key to happy, healthy children!

- If you have any concerns about your children's health or wellbeing, speak to your GP, health visitor or school nurse. If they can't help you, they will be able to suggest an alternative.

- You will find more information about health, wellbeing and your family routine in chapters 3 and 6 of this book.

Summing Up

Your children need you more now than they ever have before. If their absent parent wants to have contact with them, try and find a way that this can work that suits everyone. It's not always easy to see the person you might still be in love with, or who makes you angry, but you have to put your feelings aside and think of your children and what is best for them and what they want.

There is help and support available for people in your situation. Relate offers excellent support, counselling and advice for families who are experiencing changes (see help list for contact details).

Try and keep an honest and open dialogue with your children wherever possible, but don't overload them with worries and stresses that are yours. It's unfair of adults to blame children for their own difficulties, but often it's difficult not to - particularly if you do not have anyone else to share your problems with.

It's really important that your children know they can trust you and talk to you about their worries, whether their concerns are to do with school, their parents or their friends. Make sure they know that they can talk to you about anything at any time.

Chapter Three

Managing Your Home

If you have been living as a family and a couple you will have been used to dividing up all household chores and duties. However, now you are on your own, you will have to rethink your old routine and start planning for how you will manage your home as a single parent.

The first thing to remember is that your priority should not be the cleanliness or tidiness of your home. Although you may think it's really important, there will be other things that demand a lot of your time and energy; a little bit of dust or an unmade bed will soon become very low down on your list of priorities!

Although housework doesn't need to be your reason for living, there is no doubt that certain things do have to be done. Living in an untidy and disorganised environment is not healthy and can become quite stressful, therefore we need to find some balance between being a domestic god or goddess and having a life!

In this chapter you will find some basic, simple advice for managing your home, keeping on top of basic things like maintenance and what do to in an emergency. The first thing to do is to try and organise a family rota so that even the youngest member of the household can help with simple tasks.

Getting organised!

If you are living in a home surrounded by children's toys, dirty laundry and a sink full of washing up then chances are you are either not coping very well or you just don't care. Either way, keeping your home in a basically clean and tidy state is achievable - it doesn't have to be a show home and it doesn't have to be stressful, it's all a matter of being as organised as you possibly can.

Getting into a routine of folding laundry and putting it away, washing up and encouraging the children to tidy their toys up before bed are all simple tasks. If everyone pulls together to help, it will make a big difference to the way you live. It also means that you are not entirely responsible for everything, and spreading the load, even a little bit, will help you as well.

A family or house rota is a great way to start. Keep it simple and just list all the days of the week and what has to happen on each day. Many of the jobs will be the same, but there will be weekly tasks such as putting out the bins, cleaning out the rabbit and vacuuming the car. These can all be shared out and everyone can take it in turns to do their bit. List everyone's name on the chart as well and make it clear who will be responsible for what.

Chances are that your army of helpers may consist of children who are still quite young, so obviously you can't expect too much of them. However, even learning to put their shoes away tidily and hang up their coats and school bags will really help keep things under control, and it means there is one less thing for you to worry about.

Children's bedrooms can be a source of immense stress for parents, and teenagers seem to be the worst offenders! If your budget will stretch, it might be a good idea to offer incentives for a weekly clean up operation, either with the promise of cold, hard cash or a treat such as a takeaway. Obviously it would be far more positive for everyone to just pull together as a team and help, recognising the need for jobs to be done and your home to be kept tidy. This may work, but in reality you may have a battle on your hands, so think laterally!

De-cluttering is something that we should all try and do regularly. Instead of having a big clear out twice a year and ending up with bin bags full of stuff everywhere, take advantage of local recycling facilities, charity shops, jumble sales, car boot sales and eBay, and get rid of anything that is taking up valuable space on a regular basis. Freecycle is another excellent service that puts people in touch with each other and finds homes for unwanted goods (www.freecycle.com).

You might even find that the stuff you don't need any more can make you a bit of extra cash. You can sell things through eBay, a car boot sale or a table top sale.

■ If the housework is piling up and you are working all day and just can't physically do everything yourself, then it is time to take action.

- If your children are old enough to understand, call a family meeting and explain why you are tired and stressed and ask them to help you.

- Draw up a family rota with tasks, days of the week and everyone's name clearly marked on it. When each task has been done, tick it off because this makes you feel really good!

- If your children are very young and you are finding things really difficult, ask a friend for help. Perhaps once a week they could help you organise your house and you could do the same for them.

- A tidy, clean house is a pleasant and stress-free place to live, but none of us are perfect and you must not put yourself under unnecessary pressure in the pursuit of being perfect because it just won't happen. Your friends and family will understand if they turn up and the breakfast dishes still haven't been washed - they are coming to see you, not to inspect your house!

Maintenance and household repairs

If your partner was always the one who made arrangements for regular maintenance and household repairs to be carried out, then this is obviously something that you will now need to consider.

Major household repairs that occur as a result of an accident should all be covered by your house and contents insurance. Make sure that this is all up-to-date and if it isn't then renew it immediately.

It's very easy to forget about things and put things off when it comes to household maintenance, particularly if there are likely to be high costs and lots of disruption involved. However, the longer you leave that dripping tap, leaky roof or loose fencing panel, the worse they will get. If you really don't have a budget for things like this, in the early days of single parenting you will just have to ask friends and family for help. They will be happy to oblige - usually in return for a bit of baby-sitting or the odd meal!

If you are living in a house that needs a lot of attention and the sight of chipped paintwork, broken roof tiles and that tumbledown shed is really starting to get to you, make a plan of action and tackle one thing at a time. You will get there in the end!

'You might even find that the stuff you don't need any more can make you a bit of extra cash if you sell things through eBay, a car boot sale or a table top sale.'

- Make a list of any repairs or maintenance that your home needs and prioritise. Put all those things that really need urgent attention at the top and deal with them first.

- Work out a budget for regular maintenance that is manageable. If you have a house with a large garden that needs a lot of work to keep in shape, now could be the time to rethink and redesign it slightly to make it easier to maintain. Lots of garden maintenance companies will offer free advice.

- Don't be afraid to ask for favours. Undoubtedly, there will be lots of tasks that you can carry out yourself without any problem at all, but there are bound to be repairs that you simply can't manage on your own.

- Keep a contact list of companies or individuals who can help you with anything from fitting a new TV aerial to cleaning your carpets, servicing your boiler or sweeping the chimney.

- Keep a note of any forthcoming house maintenance in your diary or on the family calendar, e.g. when the boiler is due for a service or when you need a delivery of coal or oil for your central heating.

What to do in an emergency

Pipes do burst, roofs leak and central heating systems do break down from time to time, so it is really important to keep an up-to-date list of emergency numbers in case disaster strikes.

Keep the list by the main phone in the house and keep entries of all the numbers in your mobile as well. Keep this list updated regularly. If you look in the phone book you will find a list of emergency contact numbers for people who supply water, gas, electricity and so on.

- If something does go wrong, try not to panic. Children need to be kept safe and calm and well away from any potential dangers. Isolate the area where the problem has occurred and if necessary turn off any mains electricity.

- Ring the appropriate contact from your list, but also phone a friend or family member to come and sit with the children while you get things sorted.

- In the event of a water tank leaking or any pipes bursting there will be potentially a lot of water damage to your home. As soon as possible, contact your insurance company and start getting quotes for repairs.

- None of us can plan for any eventuality, but if you can have a small amount of savings or an emergency credit card to pay for unforeseen bills, this will take the pressure off slightly.

Emergency contact list

Organisation	Contact name	Contact number
Water board Plumber		
Electricity provider Local electrician		
Telephone / Internet provider		
Local hospital and A and E Dept		
Doctor		
Gas Board Gas Engineer		
AA / RAC / Green Flag Local garage		
Details of reliable family members/friends who are nearby and can be contacted to look after children/offer lifts in an emergency		

'Pipes do burst, roofs leak and central heating systems do break down from time to time, so it is really important to keep an up-to-date list of emergency numbers in case disaster strikes.'

You will have your own contacts to add to the list or you can add in your contact details in the space provided.

Shall I move or stay?

Suddenly finding yourself alone in the home that you once shared with your partner affects everyone differently. There will be days when you can't stand the thought of leaving and others when all you want to do is pack your bags and start afresh somewhere else.

The important thing to remember is that it is still early days and your emotions are very raw and liable to change on a daily basis. If you can accept this it will be easier to make decisions for the future.

'If at all possible, try and stay in the home that your children are familiar with as this could help them to cope with the changes you are all going through.'

Leaving your family home may not necessarily be in your hands, so unfortunately you may not have a choice. If your partner has been paying the rent or mortgage and refuses to carry on, you may have to make alternative plans. However, take legal advice as soon as possible because there is a lot of help available. Start with your local Citizens Advice Bureau because they have a wealth of information and contact details for organisations that will be able to guide you through the process of staying in your home or finding alternative accommodation.

If at all possible, try and stay in the home that your children are familiar with as this could help them to cope with the changes you are all going through. Try and give yourselves some time to adjust to your new situation before you make any big decisions. Look at your options. These could include:

- Staying in your home with the rent or mortgage paid by your former partner.
- Staying in your home and paying for it yourself by going back to work or working more hours.
- Applying for housing benefit and other benefits that can help you at a time like this.
- Moving in to Local Authority rented accommodation.
- Moving in with family or friends for a while.

Your home is important, so take time to make decisions about where you and your children will live from now on. Consider where the children go to school, your support network and how you will get to work if you decide to move out of the area.

Take as much advice as possible so that you can weigh up all your options. If you have a mortgage, contact your lender as soon as possible to explain your change in circumstances.

Talk to your children, your family and your friends and explain your situation.

Plan a household budget that includes your mortgage/rent, running costs and food bills, and stick to it! If you have a budget and a plan written down, it will make things easier to manage and will give you a proper focus.

A family rota

Throughout this book you will find references to being organised, asking for help and planning. Making lists and keeping tabs on every aspect of your life is really important and will really help you to get back in control and keep on top of things.

If you are not the most organised person in the world, the very thought of being highly efficient and planning your days might seem a bit excessive and overwhelming. However, setting aside some time every day to plan and organise your life will pay dividends!

The first stage is to decide whether you will use a diary or a wall planner or both. Make a list of everyone in the house, the days of the week and the tasks that have to happen.

Call a family meeting and discuss with the children how it's all going to work. As mentioned previously in this chapter - offer incentives if necessary!

- A wall planner in the kitchen is a good way to decide on what has to be done when and who will do it. It can be a simple piece of paper with lists or a chart - just make sure it is visible so that nobody wriggles out of their jobs!

- Keep a household diary that contains details of everything that everyone is doing every day and jobs that need to be done, including things like getting the car serviced and organising someone to help with the garden.

- Have a time every weekend when you blitz the house. If the children are old enough, insist that every Saturday morning for example, before they go out and play with their friends, they tidy their bedrooms and put all their dirty laundry in the wash.

- Divide all the household chores equally between everyone in the house. Even the youngest child can put away their Lego after they have been playing with it.

- Nobody likes housework, but letting it all build up can be stressful. A little bit of forward planning and co-operation can go a long way to creating a happy, stress-free and tidy home.

An example

Opposite is an example of how to set out a family rota.

Simply allocate one of the jobs from the bottom row to each day. For example, on Monday Sam will be responsible for hovering duties. Obviously everyone has different chores that need to be attended to, but this is useful as a guide so that you can create your own family rota. At the end of each week children can be rewarded with pocket money or a treat for helping out. They will soon be falling over themselves to help out!

Family Rota

	Monday	Tuesday	Wednesday	Thursday	Friday	Saturday	Sunday
Parent			Clean bathroom				
Sam	Hoover						
Joe		Wash up					
JOBS	**Wash up**	**Put out laundry**	**Tidy bedrooms**	**Clean bathroom**	**Clean out hamster**	**Hoover**	**Put ironing away**

Summing Up

Normal families don't live in show homes and nobody is perfect. If everyone pitches in and helps a little bit though, you can have a happy, tidy, clean and organised home. Giving children a bit of responsibility makes them feel like they are really helping and takes a bit of the load off you as well.

A routine is really important and although it sounds boring and might be the last thing you want to concern yourself with, if you have regularity with mealtimes, household chores, homework and bedtimes you will find that all the stuff that has to be done, is done. This leaves you time at weekends and in the evenings to relax and spend time together as a family.

Consider starting a family planner chart, offering rewards to children for helping out and planning a special treat at the end of the month - provided all chores have been finished of course!

Chapter Four

Finances

Most single parents have, at one time or another, had worries about money. Becoming a single parent, whatever the route into lone parenthood, inevitably causes questions to be raised about finances.

Becoming a single parent can be a scary, overwhelming and difficult experience and is high on the list of stressful and life changing events. However, with the right support it is possible to emerge from this period stronger both emotionally and financially.

Money is often the last thing anyone wants to deal with during such an emotional and tumultuous period, yet it is essential to pay careful and close attention to the financial details of any potential divorce settlement, as well as looking at your own finances in detail.

In this chapter I will try to be informative and helpful about money, explaining how to get it, how not to get into debt and offering money saving tips. There's even a section on pocket money because we all feel the pinch most when our kids tell us that everyone else gets much more than them.

'Becoming a single parent, whatever the route into lone parenthood, inevitably causes questions to be raised about finances.'

Prioritise

For many people it is often the first time in years that they have had to deal with their finances on their own. It is important to have the confidence and the knowledge that you are capable of looking after your money, and to feel secure in your ability to look after yourself financially.

In some cases one partner may have left the family finances to the other and there may be complicated investment portfolios and pension arrangements to untangle and divide, which can be difficult to understand.

Taking non-judgemental advice about money is very important, and learning how to handle one's finances alone is a big step on the road to independence. It is usually better to side-step well meaning family and friends who want to 'help' and 'advise' their relatives with the financial aspects of divorce and take independent professional advice instead.

Starting a new life after divorce is a time of new beginnings. It is an opportunity to re-evaluate your hopes and dreams for the future. Taking control financially can be very empowering and helps re-build your self-esteem and confidence. One of the most important steps you can take is to understand how to make the money you have work for you.

Get organised

- Make a list of all your bank accounts and any financial products you have such as pensions, life assurance or savings and ISAs.

- Get all your bank statements organised and in date order.

- Never ever leave any statements, letters or bills unopened - make this a new rule and stick to it. It's much better to know what you owe.

- Start to organise your family household budget by listing all the major expenditure; typically car, shopping, fuel, rent and mortgage.

- Start to get into the habit of keeping a note of everything you spend. You'll be amazed at how helpful this can be.

Talk to your bank manager

Banks - we either love them or hate them, depending on whether we are in the black or the red! Either way, if you have just become a single parent, it's a really good idea to make an appointment to see your bank manager so that you can explain your new situation to them.

If you have serious financial commitments and need help to pay loans, overdrafts or credit cards, your bank manager will be able to advise you on the best possible way forward. Before you make any decisions about restructuring your finances, talk to your bank first - do not be tempted by loan companies. Banks will often have a budget calculator that you can fill in to help you work out where you can make some savings.

- Get organised and file all your bank details in one place.

- Make a plan before you go to the bank so that you are clear about your situation.

- Be honest - if you can't work any more than you are or you think you may have to work less, tell your bank manager and explain why.

- Bank managers are human! If you give them the full story they will listen and will always try to help you.

Don't panic

Worrying about lack of money or debt is soul-destroying; it can cause sleeplessness, stress and depression. Anyone who has ever worked with single parents dreads the requests for advice that begin with 'my washing machine has broken down and I have no money' or 'my child needs a bed and it's all I can do to pay the gas bill'.

Knowing that they're doing their best trying to wash clothes out by hand or paying a whole week's food money into a launderette is painful to think back to - many of us have been there. It is so easy to fall into debt. When you need a big household item or a birthday present for your child, the catalogues and loan agencies are sorely tempting even though you know it's going to be a struggle to pay them back.

Although we all need a certain amount of money to live on, there are ways to stay in control of your finances without making panic decisions.

- Go to the library and borrow a book that can help you. Alvin Hall's *Your Money or Your Life* is brilliant and will give you lots of advice and help.

- Be sensible. If you are paying a mortgage or rent then you might be entitled to Housing Benefit. Contact your Local Authority to find out.

- If you are trying to struggle through on a very low income you might also be entitled to income support as well as Family Tax Credits.

'Although we all need a certain amount of money to live on, there are ways to stay in control of your finances without making panic decisions.'

- If you have been left without money or are waiting for earnings or benefits to come through, you may be able to get a crisis loan from Job Centre Plus. You do not have to be on benefits to apply, but the agency will need to see evidence to support your request. If you have been left without essential household items, for example bedding or cooking utensils, you may be eligible for a Community Care Grant.

The National Debtline on 0808 808 4000 (freephone) can advise anyone in the UK on debt, including bank, credit card, mortgage arrears, council tax, catalogues, hire purchase and utility debts. Issues dealt with include county court, refusal of credit, benefits, bankruptcy, bank charges, harassment, housing, homelessness and bailiffs. They provide self-help information packs and a range of factsheets.

The Citizen's Advice Bureau (CAB) can always offer advice on welfare rights, money and debt. They are spread evenly around the UK - look in your local phone book or call the Single Parents Action Network (SPAN) to find your nearest CAB. You may also have a local community advice or welfare rights service.

The Family Welfare Association (FWA) can help anyone living in the UK who is in need of financial assistance at a time of crisis in their lives. They will help with clothing (particularly children's), fuel bills and household needs such as beds, cookers, washing machines, etc. They cannot help with rent arrears, council tax, fines, funeral expenses, private school fees, repayment of social fund loans or expenses already covered by statutory funds. Applications must be made by a professional person such as a social worker, health visitor or by a voluntary agency, for example your local CAB. Average payments are £100 - £200.

FWA also runs an Educational Grants Advisory Service (EGAS); students encountering difficulties during their course can make applications. Applications must be supported by a reference from a course tutor. The student is provided with as much information as possible on other appropriate sources of finance before being referred to the Grants Service for consideration. See help list for contact details or visit www.fwa.org.uk.

The Family Service Units (FSU) works with families in need living in the inner cities of England and Scotland. If an FSU social worker feels that a family using the service is in need of a capital grant (up to £300) they will apply to FSU head office on the family's behalf. To find out if there is an FSU in your area, call 0207 402 5175.

For a booklet called 'Money to Learn (Financial Help for Adults in Further Education and Training)' call DfEE Publications Centre on 0845 602 2260 and quote reference MTLC.

Lone Parent Helpline - One-Parent Families/Gingerbread - call 0800 018 5026 (freephone) from England, Scotland or Wales for advice on maintenance, benefits and other money matters and key issues you face as a lone parent.

Single Parents in Northern Ireland can call Gingerbread for advice regarding benefits, money or debt on 0808 808 8090 (freephone).

Single Parent Action Network continues to campaign to alleviate the poverty faced by single-parent families. Visit www.singleparents.org.uk for further information.

Planning and budgeting

Having to count every penny isn't fun, but for a short time it may be essential to get yourself back on track and in control. Keeping a spending diary is important and keeping a regular check on all your direct debits and standing orders is important too. Chances are that you could instantly save some money by cancelling some that are not essential.

Have a look at service providers for things like utilities, mobile phone and Internet usage. If you have access to the Internet, check out some price comparison sites and you may be able to switch providers and save some money.

Try to pay all your bills on time and stay within your overdraft limit. This is not always possible, but you will be charged if you make payments late and this can also affect your credit rating.

If you pay a mortgage you may be entitled to a short mortgage holiday. This means that you can ask your lender to give you a break of up to six months. During this time you don't have to make your monthly repayments, but you will find that your payments increase when the payments start again.

Budget calculator

This simple budget calculator will help you work out how much money you have available each month. It will only take five minutes to complete and will really help you balance your books each month. Be as honest as you can because this will give you a clear overview of your finances and help you to plan. You can photocopy this page or just fill it in here.

Income	£
Pay after tax	
Pensions State benefits	
Interest	
Investments	
Child maintenance	
Other	
Total:	

Household spending	£
Food	
Mortgage/rent	
Council Tax	
Phone/Internet	
Water	
Other	
Total:	

Financial products spending	£
Loans/payment cards	
Pension contributions	
Savings/investments	
Life Insurance	
Other	
Total:	

Leisure spending	£
Going out	
Alcohol/cigarettes	
TV license/Satellite TV	
Holidays	
Other	
Total:	

Children	£
Childcare	
School trips School uniforms School lunches After school club fees	
Other	
Total:	

Travel	£
Getting to work Bus fare Train fare Season ticket	
Car running costs Petrol Tax Insurance Maintenance	
Other	
School bus fares	
Total:	

There is lots of help available on the Internet to really assist you with your finances. One of the best websites is www.moneysavingexpert.com. Run by financial journalist Martin Lewis, all the advice is free and can help you manage debts, save money and find out about free products and services that are available. Martin is famous for leading the campaign to help people recover their bank charges and produces a weekly e-newsletter that anyone can sign up for.

Checklist

- Always go shopping on a full stomach.

- Go shopping with cash and only spend what you've got.

- Write down everything you spend so that over a period of time you can monitor where your money actually goes.

- Keep a small extra float so that you have enough to take advantage of those 3 for the price of 2 offers.

- Do not leave electrical items on standby - it means they are still using electricity. Turn them off and unplug your mobile phone charger too!

- Check out which evening the cinema has a cheap night (usually mid week) and see the film then - also buy popcorn and drinks in the supermarket before you go.

- Turn the heating off half an hour earlier, put a jumper on and snuggle up on the sofa under a blanket (kids love this - camping in the living room!).

- Always check your till receipt and change - mistakes are made more often than you think.

- It can feel like purgatory when you're scrimping and saving all of the time - if you are saving for something (a holiday, a new sofa, a groovy pair of shoes) put a picture of it on your fridge. It makes it all feel worth it and is something to look forward to.

Summing Up

If you end up wondering why there's so much month left at the end of the money try doing a detailed budget to find out where it all goes.

Start by keeping a note of everything you spend for a month. Chances are you'll be splashing the cash on all kinds of stuff you hadn't expected. Everybody's different, but you may find that you are spending more than you think on some items.

Next, make a list of all the things you need to pay for every month. Remember to include a realistic amount for entertainment and socialising; don't force yourself to live like a hermit.

A good tip is to add 10% to your total expected outgoings. There are always unexpected extras such as birthdays, children's shoes or car repairs to pay for. This should allow for them and smooth over the shock of any nasty surprises.

If the final amount you need to spend in an average month is more than you have coming in, have a look at the spending and see if you can make any economies. If you're lucky enough to have money left over you can put some by each month for bigger items, provided you actually stick to your budget of course.

If there is a large deficit in your budget each month you may need to seek advice about managing debt.

Chapter Five

Working

You may have already been working and have done so since your children were born, having returned to work following a period of maternity leave. Alternatively, becoming a single parent may have left you with no option but to return to work or find a different job that can accommodate your new situation.

It is a fact that there are more working parents in the UK now than ever before, so be assured that if you do decide to return to work, you won't be alone. In fact, you may well find that you make up the majority of your workforce, rather than the minority.

There is an increasing amount of help and support available for working parents and you may find that your employer is particularly sympathetic to your needs. However, you may also find that you struggle to get what you want in terms of flexible working hours, so this chapter will try and give you some ideas and possible solutions.

Working and being a parent basically means that you have two full time jobs. Many part time workers find they are doing a full time job in part time hours, and it is a well known fact that parents can often do eight hours of work in five. There are various job options available to you, ranging from part time, term time office work to running your own business from home, so you are bound to find something that will suit you.

Keeping your job

If you are already working and then become a single parent, it is a good idea to let your employer know as soon as possible. You may need to take some time off, either in holiday that you are owed or unpaid leave if you have a lot of issues to sort out and resolve. Becoming a single parent is an exhausting and emotional roller coaster and you may simply need time off to adjust and get used to your new situation.

Turning up for work tired, emotional and unable to cope will not ingratiate yourself with your boss or work mates. Although everyone will understand to a point, it is probably a much better idea to take some time off until you feel completely able to cope again.

Reasonable employers will understand how hard things are for you and make allowances. If your boss doesn't appear to have the first idea of what you are going through, consider asking a colleague for help and support and ask them to talk to your boss on your behalf.

'There is an increasing trend for people to work from home, either as an employee of a larger company or as the owner of their own company.'

If things still do not seem to be improving you will either have to pull yourself together and get on with it (easier said than done, and in many cases almost impossible) or look for another job that can accommodate the needs of you and your children.

- If necessary, write a letter to your employer informing them of your new situation.

- If you need time off - take it. There is no need to feel guilty. You may well have a blossoming career, but your children need you more than ever at the moment and they have to come first. You may have to put your ambitions on hold for a while.

- Under EU employment law you can apply for flexible working conditions. Your boss has to consider your application, although there is no guarantee that you will be given flexibility. If you have a trade union representative, seek their advice.

- If your current job won't or can't accommodate your new needs it might be time to look elsewhere.

Taking a career break

This could be the best thing you ever do because having a complete break from work for a while will give you plenty of breathing space to sort out your plan of action.

If you are in the fortunate position of receiving a decent amount of maintenance, or have savings or funds from other sources that can tide you over, then you are in a strong position to have a career break.

However, even if you don't have funds behind you, you should consider a break from work and investigate the possibility of claiming Income Support or Jobseekers Allowance for a while.

As a single parent you will also be entitled to Lone Parent Benefit. Lots of information about the benefits you are entitled to can be found on the Internet. See the help list at the back of the book for web addresses.

Things to consider

- Having a break from work doesn't mean you are giving up and is not a sign of failure, weakness or inability to cope. It is a sensible move at a stressful time in your life.

- Consider claiming benefits for a while. If you have paid National Insurance for most of your working life you are entitled to help when you need it the most.

- While you are having a break, use the time effectively to plan your life strategy, but don't put yourself under unnecessary pressure to make decisions too quickly. With a bit of time and thought you will be able to find a way to carry on working and looking after your children.

Re-starting your career

If you have not been working for a while because your partner worked and you brought up the children, this may be the point that you need to consider returning to work.

Taking a long break from work can bring potential problems to light and it is best not to rush headlong into anything. You may find that the workplace has changed quite a lot since you last worked and that your skills may need updating before you even start to look for a job.

'It is a fact that there are more working parents in the UK now than ever before, so be assured that if you do decide to return to work, you won't be alone.'

There is help available for those returning to work - your local Job Centre Plus will have plenty of information about workshops and courses that you can attend, and many of them will be free.

Going back to work is not that easy when you have children to consider and we will look at childcare in detail at the end of this chapter. However, it can be done with careful planning and by finding a sensible job option that allows you to work during school hours.

'Going out to work, getting ready and being in a different, grown up environment that doesn't revolve around kids, telly and finger painting can be really good for your self-esteem and confidence - as well as your bank balance!'

What to look for

- Don't be put off if you haven't worked for a while. There is help available and you will soon get your confidence back. Enlist the help of good friends to help you with everything from updating your CV to what to wear for your interview.

- Looking for jobs that specifically give you flexible hours may limit your options. However, if you see a job that is perfect and matches your skills and experience it is always worth asking about job sharing or flexi time.

- Be sensible and don't apply for jobs that will stress you out. There is nothing worse than taking a job because you need the money and hating every minute of it. That won't benefit you or your family.

- Think about school holidays, the school day and the fact that children do get sick from time to time and need to be at home. Try and find a job that will allow for these eventualities, otherwise you may find yourself paying out a large chunk of your salary in childcare.

Working from home and starting a business

There is an increasing trend for people to work from home, either as an employee of a larger company or as the owner of their own company. Working freelance is a good way to try and get some work/life balance into your situation and can be a great way to work around your children without having to rely too much on childcare.

If your job allows you to work from home for even part of the week, this may be the perfect solution. However, if you have pre-school children you will still have to use childcare because it will be almost impossible to be at all productive with little children around!

If your children are of school age, working from home can make for a virtually stress-free career option if you are happy with your own company and have the motivation and dedication to make it work.

You do have to employ a strict regime and plan your work day properly though, otherwise you will find that your house soon becomes a drop-in centre for all your friends and you will never get any work finished on time.

If you want to work from home, why not ask your boss if this is a possibility. Many employers are happy to consider home working as an option as it keeps their overheads lower and it is a fact that many people who work from home are more productive than if they were in an office environment.

Starting your own business and running it from home is another option and there are some excellent books and websites that specialise in this subject. It is probably best to keep your ideas simple, for example if you were working as a journalist on a newspaper before you became a single parent, now might be a good time to consider going freelance and setting up in business on your own providing freelance journalism and copywriting services.

Developing new products and services costs time and money and should not be discounted, but should be considered carefully before you take the plunge. Many people find that they want to run a small business and start doing this on a part time basis first, eventually jumping ship after a year or two when things have really started to take off.

- If you want to work from home make sure you are properly set up to do so. You will need a space in your home that you can call your own. You will need a PC, desk space, a phone line and room to store files and work-related information.

- Make sure you let your friends and family know that when you are working you are not available for socialising. Start as you mean to go on!

- Get organised! Make sure you have an office diary, a filing system and childcare all sorted before you even begin to join the home working revolution that is sweeping the UK.

- Starting your own business is hard work and requires commitment and a certain level of support. Having ideas is great, but following them through can be quite another thing. With small children at your feet and no full time support this could prove stressful. Take your time!

- Working from home can be a great way to enable you to be there for your children. You don't have to worry about the school run, school holidays or what to do if your child is poorly.

Getting some advice

As this book went to press, we were in the grip of a credit crunch with many people losing their jobs through redundancies. More than three million people in the UK already work from home, so if you have been faced with redundancy then working from home could be a good option for you.

There is plenty of advice available through Business Link (www.businesslink.org.uk), the government agency that exists to help people start and run small businesses. The website www.enterprisenation.com is also full of help and advice for home workers, and was founded by Emma Jones, an experienced home business owner.

One of the newest resources for anyone who works from home is Habmag (www.habmag.com).This is a weekly e-newsletter and website that provides news and features to home entrepreneurs. The e-newsletter costs around £1 a week but includes special offers, discounts and competitions to win home office equipment.

Key points to consider when starting a new business

- Are you developing a new product or service? If you are then seek advice from an organisation such as Business Link who will help you with business plans.

- Working from home can be lonely! Make sure you get out and network at least once a week.

- Do what makes you happy and what you know about.

- Accept help and advice willingly. Keep a list of everyone you speak to - you never know when you might need them.

'Working from home was the best move I made. I have flexibility and know that if there is a problem with one of my children I can be there at the drop of a hat. Cashflow can be a nightmare when people don't pay their bills on time, but the pros outweigh the cons for me.' Jo, 42, home entrepreneur and mum to two children.

Childcare

Finding a new job, re-starting your career, working from home or starting a business is all well and good, but if you don't have decent childcare in place you will find life becomes even harder than it is already.

If you have very young children, you may find that your Local Education Authority uses the nursery voucher scheme and that you only need to pay a reduced rate for your childcare. Your local providers will be able to advise you about this, as the system varies from region to region across the UK.

If you are working full time, traditionally a private nursery place or the services of a full time childminder, nanny or *au pair* would probably have been the most sensible options. However, if you are returning to work in order to bring a decent amount of money home each week, it is pretty pointless to spend the majority of your hard earned cash on childcare. You may find that even with the cost of childcare you are still able to provide an enhanced standard of living for yourself and your children - if that is the case, then you are very fortunate!

If things are not quite that simple, but you need to work and have some childcare, there are other options. If you work part time perhaps you could arrange to do a childcare swap with another working parent. Many workplaces have crèche facilities or have secured really good deals with local nursery providers for their employees, so it is worth asking the question. If your company doesn't do this, ask why it is and see if you can start the ball rolling. You will then be helping other working parents as well as yourself.

If you can make an arrangement with a local childminder who will take care of your children in their home while you work, this can be a great option - particularly if there are other children present at the same time. Alternatively, ask for help from your family. The only danger with this option is that they have to understand that the arrangement is permanent and will have to happen at the same time each week.

- Consider childcare when applying for jobs, but don't be put off going for a job because of it. There is always a way around every situation - it's just a case of being a bit creative sometimes!

- Breakfast clubs, after school clubs and holiday play schemes are great for children. They get to spend time doing different things and mixing with different children. However, bear in mind the age of your children, particularly when you look at before and after school clubs. Very young children may find a week of early starts to be quite a punishing regime after a while.

- Share childcare costs with friends. A nanny or childminder share scheme can work really well as it splits the cost evenly and your children get to play with their friends while you work.

- Get into the habit of sharing school runs - even before you go back to work. This gets everyone used to the new regime before your new job begins. Perhaps you can also do after school childcare swaps with the same parent.

- If you work a certain number of hours each week you are entitled to claim Working Families Tax Credit, Lone Parent Benefit and Child Tax Credit. You are also entitled to claim for childcare costs as long as the childcare provider is registered with the Local Authority.

Summing Up

Working as a single parent will not always be easy but it doesn't have to be stressful either and can be a really positive move.

Going out to work, getting ready and being in a different, grown up environment that doesn't revolve around kids, telly and finger painting can be really good for your self-esteem and confidence - as well as your bank balance!

If you are happy then your children will be too. If you have to leave them with a childminder make it into a big adventure and make sure they are in a setting that makes them feel happy and secure; there is nothing worse than leaving a sad, crying child and racing to work. It may take you a while to find the right solution for all of you, but this is just part of the process of being a working single parent.

Remember that being a working single parent will be very different to your working life before children or when you were married and it is best to accept this from the start. Trying to be as dynamic, ambitious and available as you were in your previous life will just put you under unnecessary pressure to be a super parent - it's just not realistic!

Balance is the most important element of being a working parent. Try not to bring work home with you and if you have to, wait until the children are in bed before you even attempt to finish it. If you work from home, switch your laptop and mobile off between 4pm and bedtime. Trying to work while your children are demanding after school snacks and help with homework will only end in misery!

Chapter Six

Health and Wellbeing

Parenting is hard work - there is no doubt about it. This is compounded if you suddenly find yourself as a single parent and are trying to juggle work, running a home, managing finances and bringing up your children with little or no support.

It is very easy to neglect your own needs when you have so many other things to think about, but you can only keep running at full capacity for so long before you collapse in a heap.

Even something as simple as sitting down with your children and enjoying a relaxing meal will make you feel better and is a good way to end the day, giving everyone a chance to forget about school and work and catch up.

It is really important to try and take care of yourself. Even though you may feel that there is simply no time for you in your daily schedule, there are lots of ways to improve your health and wellbeing that can help you stay positive about your situation.

Building in some time for exercise, even if it is just a walk around the block at lunchtime to get some fresh air, can make you feel better and more focused. If you have been used to meeting friends and playing sport once or twice a week, it might be difficult to continue these regular events. However, try and maintain contact with your friends and the activity you enjoy - just think about scaling things back for a while until you have a routine in place that can support this.

Managing stress and finding time for yourself at the end of a long and busy day can make you feel better about yourself, even if this just means lighting some candles and relaxing in a hot bath with a glass of wine or enjoying a

'It is so easy to forget about yourself when you are manically busy, but it is so important to make sure that you take care of yourself because if you don't, nobody else will.'

Helen Taylor, physiotherapist, 44.

favourite film or TV programme. Listening to music, reading the paper and chatting to friends on the phone or over the Internet are also good ways to maintain a balance in your life.

Getting a good night's sleep sounds simple, but with very young children this can be almost impossible. You may find that you occasionally need to have some very early nights to recuperate.

Looking after yourself

Exercise

Exercise may well be the last thing on your mind, but there is no need to find the idea of a brisk 20 minute walk or a half hour swim at lunchtime daunting. We all know that regular exercise makes us feel better and is good for our overall wellbeing. However, it should be fun and part of your daily routine so that it doesn't become a chore.

The British Heart Foundation says: 'Being physically active will help keep your heart healthy as well as providing other health benefits. People who are not physically active have an increased risk of heart disease and latest statistics suggest that seven out of 10 adults do not take enough exercise. It is never too late to start and being active does not mean you have to join a gym or an exercise class, but it could include fitting in walking or swimming to your daily routine.'

Good circulation is a major key to maintaining good health and we are not designed to sit around for long periods of time. It's not just the heart, lungs and muscles that benefit from exercise - exercise is vital for whole body health. Try to avoid sitting in one place for too long; at work take regular breaks and at home get down on the floor and play with your children.

Regular exercise will make you feel good. When endorphins are released they can produce a sense of general wellbeing and you may find that you get a buzz after your exercise session that will help manage stress, induce a good night's sleep and make you feel better about yourself. Exercise can be good for depression and also makes you focus, so try and build at least 10 minutes a day into your schedule.

Soon you will find that you don't even notice you are exercising. Walks in the park with babies in pushchairs and bike rides with the children will help all of you to stay healthy, as well as being a fun way to spend time together.

- Getting out and about and getting fresh air is an important part of your health and wellbeing.

- By working out on a regular basis your body becomes more efficient at burning calories. This also gives you more energy throughout the day.

- Increased exercising leads to a strengthening of the immune system, which means you are less prone to illness. Single parents can't afford to be ill!

- Stress levels can be reduced by regular workouts.

- A regular exercise slot gives structure to your day, which is really important.

Diet and nutrition

A busy and challenging life can leave little or no time for spending hours in the kitchen every day, creating gourmet cuisine from scratch. Coming up with well balanced, nutritious and tasty meals for you and your family need not be a chore. With some planning and delegation, cooking can be healthy and fun.

There are lots of meals that can be prepared quickly, cheaply and easily that will provide you with a balanced diet. Gill Levett, founder of the online family meal planner www.1click2cook.com, said: 'I had the idea for the website because I was a busy mum buying a lot of packet foods. I had little time to plan in advance and thought it would be a good idea to create a website full of simple, easy to cook, well balanced recipes that would be suitable for busy mums to make for their families.'

Be wary not to forget yourself when feeding the family. Investing all your time and energy in cooking for your children, whilst neglecting your own needs, will not help you in the long run. Busy mums spend a lot of time preparing, cooking, serving and clearing up after a family meal and often find themselves jumping up and down from the table every five minutes, leaving them with little time to enjoy the meal they have spent so long cooking.

'Coming up with well balanced, nutritious and tasty meals for you and your family need not be a chore and with some planning and delegation cooking can be healthy and fun.'

Do not fall into the trap of missing dinner and grabbing late night, unhealthy snacks. Instead, try to find easy, simple recipes that can be whipped up in a few minutes. If your children are old enough, encourage them to get involved too. It's a good opportunity to catch up on the day's events and spend some time together as a family.

When planning your meals, you need to find ingredients that have high nutritional value and slow release calories to maintain consistent energy levels throughout the day.

What you need to remember

- Always try and have breakfast and encourage your children to do the same. Research has shown that children perform better at school if they have had a healthy and filling breakfast. If you are going to work and you don't have time for breakfast at home, take something with you, even if it is just a banana. This way you will avoid the fatal 10.30am chocolate or sticky bun snack attack.

- If your children have packed lunches for school, try and pack them the night before to avoid a stressful morning that could lead to a missed breakfast. Make sure they are well balanced as well as varied so your children don't get bored. It is a fact that your children will be starving when they get home from school, but healthy lunch options will help prevent extreme mood swings and help keep stress levels low.

- If you work at home, try to avoid constant trips to the biscuit tin. Keep a stock of healthy snacks in the cupboard and make sure you have a well balanced lunch that will give you enough energy to cope with the school run and beyond.

- Health experts recommend that we should all drink plenty of water and try to avoid too much caffeine, alcohol or carbonated sugary drinks. Although short term stimulants are appealing, the long term effects can be damaging to your health and will result in peaks and troughs in your energy levels.

- There are ways to encourage your family to stick to a healthy, well balanced diet .Stock up on healthy snacks, fruit, fruit juices and low calorie drinks. These are all acceptable options and after a while you will all get used to healthier living.

'If you feel good about yourself you will be a happier person and potentially a better parent. Eating well and getting plenty of sleep are really important to keep your energy levels up.'

Sarah Parker, 39, writer.

58

Dealing with stress

Stress is an almost unavoidable symptom of single parenting - or any kind of parenting! Some people seem to thrive on it, while others find it incredibly difficult to manage and eventually it can spiral out of control.

Stress makes you tired, more susceptible to illness and can affect every part of your life - from work to parenting. Your friendships may suffer and you could feel that you have the weight of the world on your shoulders.

Before life starts to get difficult to manage, there are things that you can put in place to try and keep your stress levels under control. One of the most important actions is to try and tell people close to you how you are feeling. Admitting that you are finding life difficult is not a sign of weakness or inadequacy - it is far better to be honest and open and discuss your situation.

Asking for help and accepting offers of help can be one of the hardest things you do. As a single parent you may well have reasons for proving to yourself and other people that you really can cope on your own. While this is admirable, it may not be entirely sensible.

Asserting your independence is one thing, but driving yourself into the ground will not benefit you or your children. If a friend offers to share the school runs with you so that you can get to work on time, say yes. You can always repay the favour by taking turns and sharing after school childcare.

Whether you work part time or full time, having the added pressure of bringing children up alone and not having a partner any more can have a big impact on your working life. Again, tell your boss (most are reasonable people) what is going on and see if you can come up with a plan that will mean you keep your job but perhaps have less responsibility or fewer hours for a while. It is far better to work reduced hours and keep your job than to start making mistakes and eventually lose your job. Lots of single parents work flexible hours that fit in with school days and holidays, so it is worth asking the questions.

'Asking for help and accepting offers of help can be one of the hardest things you do.'

Stress checklist

- Physical activity of any sort can reduce stress levels, so try and make time to do this regularly.

- You are important! Remember that you are allowed time off and you are not superhuman. You can't do everything yourself because nobody can, so don't beat yourself up if your house is not as tidy as usual or you burn the dinner. It really is not the end of the world and you can always buy a takeaway!

- Try and eat well. Stress can lead to depression, which can lead to comfort eating and drinking. You will only feel worse if you don't take care of yourself.

- Go and see your doctor and ask for advice for managing stress. Your GP will have access to resources and can refer you to a specialist if necessary.

- Homeopathic and complementary therapies and treatments are excellent for dealing with stress. Homeopathy encourages the body to heal itself. Anyone can use homeopathic remedies and, according to the World Health Organisation, it is the second most widely used medicine in the world.

For more information see *Stress – The Essential Guide*.

Relaxation

Finding time to really relax can be a challenge in itself and if trying to take time off is making you stressed, why not have a rethink. You may find that you need to teach yourself how to do it, as everyone has a different way of relaxing.

Meditation, yoga and prayer are often seen as traditional ways of relaxing, but if watching your favourite TV show, shopping with your girlfriends or settling down with a good book are more your thing, then that is fine.

Removing yourself from a stressful situation by doing something completely different can help you to switch off. When you have found the relaxation methods that suit you, build them into your life.

Being alone with your children is demanding and can be a lonely and seemingly thankless task at times. Relaxing and taking time off from your daily routine is not only good for you, but will also benefit your children. If your days

'Removing yourself from a stressful situation by doing something completely different can help you to switch off. When you have found the relaxation methods that suit you, build them into your life.'

always revolve around school runs, rushing to work, rushing back again and then organising after school activities for your children, you really do need to mix with other adults and break your routine. This could mean signing up for an evening class once a week and organising a regular babysitter, or simply meeting for the occasional night out and having a really good laugh with friends.

- As well as exercise, activities and nights out, listening to music is a good way to unwind. There are many CDs available that are designed specifically to de-stress and aid relaxation.

- Meditation can just mean sitting or lying down and relaxing. Taking a few minutes away from your work or a stressful situation to simply be quiet and regulate your breathing can bring huge benefits.

- Relaxation experts claim that practising creative visualisation and imagining that you are somewhere else can be very effective. Local colleges often offer courses in stress management and relaxation techniques.

- Massage is a proven technique for aiding relaxation. Many therapists offer home visits, but there are also many books and websites that offer instruction on basic massage principles.

- Aromatherapy is not just for the treatment of specific ailments and does not have to involve an expensive stay at a spa or beauty clinic. Candles and oils that promote relaxation are widely available and can be used in your own home. Put a few drops of lavender (calming, therapeutic and for the treatment of anxiety), geranium (comforting and healing) or ylang ylang (good for high blood pressure) into a hot bath, or combine with a base oil such as almond oil and massage into the skin before bedtime.

Sleep

Sleep can be a rare commodity, particularly if you have very young children or you are suffering from stress or anxiety. However, it is a fact that a good night's sleep can make a big difference to your concentration, your ability to cope with everyday life and even your tolerance levels.

Prolonged lack of sleep over a period of time can affect your general health and wellbeing, leaving you run down and open to picking up infections.

If worries are keeping you awake at night, try writing them down before you go to sleep and some ideas for possible solutions, then you know you will not forget about them.

If you wake in the night and cannot get back to sleep, get out of bed and do something else; lying there and worrying about not sleeping will make matters worse.

Tips to help

- To try and make sure you get a good night's sleep, resist the temptation to take a long nap during the day. This will throw out your body clock and will mean you will not sleep as well at night.

- Try to limit caffeine and alcohol intake and avoid eating large meals too late at night. Instead you could sip a cup of herbal tea and incorporate this into your pre-sleep ritual of trying to wind down and taking a warm bath before you go to bed.

- Expose yourself to bright light and sunlight soon after waking and keep your bedroom dark while sleeping. Keep your bedroom as a sanctuary of peace and tranquillity and try not to work in bed!

- Exercise early in the day as over exertion near to bedtime will over stimulate you.

- Try to avoid over the counter sleeping tablets at all costs as they can have an adverse effect on you during the day. If you do have a persistent sleep problem you could make an appointment with your GP.

Summing Up

The fact is that as a single parent you have no choice but to take good care of yourself - that means your physical, mental and emotional wellbeing. Nipping off to spas for relaxation breaks won't be a realistic option for everyone, so you have to grab your opportunities for 'me time' when you can and not feel guilty about it.

Serious problems involving lack of sleep, loss of appetite or overwhelming feelings of being unable to cope with life should be addressed quickly and help sought from professionals. Talk to your GP if you have any worries and they will be happy to help you.

Eat and sleep well, get fresh air, exercise and socialise with your friends; these are all important elements of taking care of your health and wellbeing. If you are worried, concerned or anxious then talk to your friends - they may not be able to solve all your problems, but having a network of people around you who you can truly trust and rely on goes a long way to helping you see clearly and find a way through any problems or difficulties.

Chapter Seven

Support Networks

One of the most important things to recognise as a single parent is that you will start to rely more on your friends and family for support. Far from this being an imposition, people will probably be expecting it and will want to help you in any way they can.

You may find that you simply need someone to talk things through with - a problem shared is a problem halved after all. Perhaps you need advice about a legal issue and someone you know is a specialist in this area, or maybe your personal finances need some attention.

Whatever the issue, you will find that someone has the knowledge, expertise or skill that you need to help you. Or you may just find that they make you laugh and see that things are really not that bad after all - sometimes laughter really is the best medicine!

In this chapter we will look at the importance of support networks, how they can help you and how you can create one if you don't have a group of friends already.

Friends and family

Your friends and family will probably be worried about you, but they may demonstrate that worry by trying to organise you and telling you what to do, which may be very difficult for you to cope with. Although they have the best of intentions, they may lose it in the delivery. Be aware of this and try to be gracious - even if they are driving you to distraction. Generally speaking, it's only because they care - honest!

'It's a good idea for your children to continue to have as much contact as possible with your family so they recognise that although their life at home has changed, their relatives are still there and they can still spend time with them when they want to.'

It's a good idea for your children to continue to have as much contact as possible with your family so they recognise that although their life at home has changed, their relatives are still there and they can still spend time with them when they want to. Make it a rule though, right from the beginning, that whatever the circumstances of your single-parent status, it is not a good idea to discuss an absent parent with the children - unless they want to.

It is always best to be led by children when it comes to discussing feelings and emotions and if you ask your family to respect your wishes there is no reason to suspect they won't.

Friends and family can be a fantastic ready made support network, but remember that they also know you very well and will feel that they can be very honest and that you won't mind. Chances are there will be days when you do, so you need to make it clear to them that you value their support, but that you also know what's best for you and your children.

If friends and family members are really proving to be a negative influence and are dragging you down by constantly talking about your situation and raking over old ground, then tell them. You need to surround yourself with positive people who will really help you and support you - not with those who will criticise you and make you feel like a failure.

If they don't take your concerns on board then it might be wise to reduce the amount of contact you have with them for a while until the dust has settled. It's important to have people around you who can help, support and advise you when necessary. Try to eliminate anyone who is negative, critical or just needy. Life as a single parent is hard enough - you don't need to make it any harder!

Tips for an easier life

- Don't pretend that everything is fine when it clearly isn't.

- If you can't rely on your closest friends and family at a time when you really need support then who can you turn to?

- Stay in control - sitting around all day with a bunch of people who just breed negativity is not productive. If people want to see you then ask them to ring before they call round.

- If you get on well with your family and your children have a good relationship with them, encourage them to have as much contact as possible.

- Don't forget about your children's friends as well. Your children need support, help and distraction as much as you do and their friends are important too.

The professionals

A lot of professional help exists to support single parents and, as this book has not been written by a counsellor, we have singled out a few of the best options available to you.

If you really feel you can't talk to your friends or family, or you have moved to a new area and you really don't know anyone yet, a good starting point is your local GP or health centre. They will be able to give you some advice and put you in touch with relevant people who can help you with different areas of your life.

For example, you may be finding it difficult to cope with bringing up your children on your own or you may need advice on going back to work, managing your finances, looking after your health and so on.

Professional counsellors, coaches and advisors are all experienced, highly trained individuals who have a detailed understanding of the problems that you are facing. They will not judge you or force you to make a decision about any of the difficulties you might be dealing with, but they will give you the opportunity to talk about everything that is worrying you.

'If you really feel you can't talk to your friends or family, or you have moved to a new area and you really don't know anyone yet, a good starting point is your local GP or health centre.'

Sometimes, the thought of talking about your feelings and worries to a complete stranger can be daunting and overwhelming, as well as very uncomfortable. Talking to counsellors and therapists about things will mean that they do ask you questions that you might struggle to answer.

It's important to be as honest and open as you possibly can. Their role is to guide you through a difficult time in your life and try and find you some solutions that will really help you in the future. It is not their job to solve all your problems for you - they will simply equip you with tools that can help you to manage your life.

What you need to do

- Therapists, counsellors, life coaches and advisors all have your interests at heart. Lots of free help is available and the best place to start is your local health centre or GP.

- If you do decide to seek professional help, do not expect miracles to happen overnight. Having counselling is a process that can take some time, but by taking this first step you will begin to rebuild your life.

- Talking to a complete stranger about your inner most thoughts and feelings is not easy for everyone. However, many people find it easier to talk to complete strangers than to their friends and family.

- When you find the counsellor that is right for you (see the next part of this chapter for some suggestions) make an appointment and stick to it. You will probably be encouraged to have weekly meetings with your counsellor, so put the date in your diary and make it part of your routine.

- Although it sounds scary, having counselling can be an essential part of your health and wellbeing and lots of people have asked for professional help. Celebrities are always happy to reveal the fact that they are seeing a therapist, so there is no reason for you to feel uncomfortable about it. Don't be scared to get help!

Organisations and groups that can help you

The one organisation that everyone has heard of is Relate. Formerly the Marriage Guidance Bureau, Relate has offices all over the country and is undoubtedly the most well known organisation that can help anyone with any element of their relationship.

There are also dozens of websites that offer online advice, forums, chat rooms, features and articles - a lot of this information is provided by experienced single parents who really know what you are going through and have experienced many of the same situations themselves and survived. If you don't have access to the Internet at home, visit your local library or cyber café.

Getting help

- At the back of this book there is a help list that contains web addresses and contact information for a selection of organisations that will be able to help you.

- A good way to find out about help and support is to join a local group that supports single parents. Most areas have groups that meet in village halls, sports centres or at other venues on a regular basis and they are a great source of support.

- Talk to your GP or health visitor about help and advice. They will have information leaflets, contact numbers and names. You may even find that a regular drop in group meets at your local health centre.

- Asking for help can be daunting and can make you feel as though you are failing. In fact, you are making positive steps to change your situation and this should be seen as a very positive achievement.

Relate is an excellent organisation and has a team of trained, qualified professional counsellors based across the UK. A spokesman said: 'Relate is for people who want to make their family relationships better. We help people make sense of what's happening in their relationships, decide what they want to do and make those changes. Relate works with couples, individuals and families at a national network of Relate Centres and via email and phone counselling.' For more information about Relate, call 0300 100 1234 or visit www.relate.org.uk.

Relate have published a book called *Help Your Children Cope with Your Divorce*, written by Paula Hall, a Relate counsellor. Visit their website for more information.

Summing Up

Becoming a single parent is a shock; your life will change quickly and dramatically. You may find that initially you are so sad, angry and upset that you operate on auto pilot for a while and just stumble through each day without giving it too much thought. You may also be so completely determined to cope and show the world that you can manage your life on your own with your children and that you don't need anyone's help at all.

However, as time goes on you may well find that things change and you become less able to cope. A big reason for this may be tiredness, but you may also need professional help at this point to help you deal with what has happened to you and to move forward.

Many single parents I spoke to when researching this book found that although the first year was the hardest in many ways, it was the second and third years of single parenting when they found they needed counsellors or other professionals to help them find a strategy for managing their feelings and coping with difficulties.

Asking for help and support from your friends and family, and perhaps later from a professional, is not a sign of weakness but an indication that you are recognising that you need some help and guidance during a very difficult time of your life.

Chapter Eight

Dating Again

When you are first on your own with your children, the last thing that you will want to think about is meeting someone new. Chances are that you are still in love with your former partner, or maybe you are so full of anger that you can't stand the thought of being close to anyone ever again.

In time, your feelings will change and there is bound to come a point when lots of well meaning people will start to make comments about finding a new partner and getting back out there and dating. It might sound easy, but it's really not that simple, particularly when you have been with the same partner for a number of years and you have young children.

Even thinking about being with a new person can be daunting and it all takes time. Some people can move on quickly and within a few months or a year find that they have met someone new and are even thinking about settling down with them.

For other people, being single becomes an almost permanent state and they find meeting new people and forming relationships really difficult for lots of reasons. Learning to trust someone again can be hard and can take time; you need to give yourself a break and take things slowly if you are unsure.

Apart from the confidence and assertiveness that is needed to go out there and meet people again, time is also a big factor.

In this chapter we will look at the practicalities of meeting new people, where to go to meet them, trusting people again and how your children can be affected by new people in your life.

'When you are first on your own with your children, the last thing that you will want to think about is meeting someone new.'

Meeting people

'I adored my husband and we had two beautiful boys. One day he just left us - with nothing. He had been having an affair with a colleague and he walked out and never came back. I was heartbroken and in pieces. Three months later I met my new husband. He delivered something to my house while I was gardening one day. It happened quickly and my family were not very supportive, but I knew he was right for me and my boys. He has two boys as well and now we all live together and we are a happily blended family. My family has accepted him and it's fine.' Jane, 44, mum to two boys and step-mum to two boys.

It sounds easy doesn't it? 'Go out and meet someone new, you're bound to bump into someone in the supermarket/pub/library...' It's so easy for someone who is already in a relationship to make assumptions that meeting your next partner will just be a stroll in the park.

So, where do you start? Firstly, make sure you are really ready to move on emotionally from your last relationship - this can take time and everyone is different. You may also find that some people are not impressed if you try and move on too quickly, but the important thing to remember is that it really isn't any of their business. As long as you are confident that you are doing the right thing at the right time for you and your children, that's all that matters.

There are lots of places where you can meet people and many people do say that the person of your dreams will walk into your life when you least expect it. However, if you have tried the school gate, supermarket queue and local pub, with no success, you can try organised dating instead.

Internet dating, speed dating, personal ads and dating agencies are everywhere. One click of a mouse and you are on the Internet with access to millions of potential partners. However, although internet dating has created many happy, safe and fulfilling relationships, there are also many horror stories from people who have had negative experiences while trying to meet people online.

'I was on a cyber date mission for about three years! I used to be obsessed with checking my inbox and surfing for potential dates. However, I learned quickly that you can be anyone you want to be on the Internet, and I just had

> 'After a while, I felt that I was ready to meet someone new, but I just found that although I liked the idea of it all, by 7pm I was exhausted and just didn't have the energy to get dressed up and go out!'
>
> Sarah, 39.

Need2Know

one disappointing experience after another. In the end I met a really nice man through a friend - it was just safer that way!' Sarah, 40, single mum for nine years.

Top tips

- If you really want to get out there and start dating again then do your homework! There are lots of books and websites available that explore this subject in a lot more detail.

- Make sure you have the confidence and assertiveness to deal with knock backs and disappointments.

- Think about the kind of person you want to meet and go to places where they might be. It's no good trying to re-invent yourself as a clubber or scuba diver in the hope that you will meet someone if you are happier seeing the latest film or walking up mountains!

- Internet dating can be fun, but can also be expensive. There are sites that are set up just for single parents which are listed at the back of the book in the help section.

- Be careful and only arrange to meet someone in broad daylight in a very public place. Make sure you tell your friends where you will be, take your mobile and ring someone to let them know you have arrived and that you are okay.

- Your date may not turn out as planned, so make sure you have a contingency plan. If things are getting awkward just excuse yourself and say you have to make a call to check on your kids. Alternatively, you could arrange for a friend to ring you at a set time. If things are getting tricky this could be your get out of jail free card!

- Don't expect miracles, but don't get too disheartened. You have to kiss a lot of frogs before you meet your prince or princess and getting out there and dating can be a great way to boost your confidence and meet new and interesting people. You may not meet your next long term partner, but you could end up with some interesting friends and some new interests, and who knows where that might lead!

Children

Children are more resilient than we think and often cope far better with changes and developments in their lives than adults do - usually because they have the ability to take everything at face value and do not over analyse situations.

Introducing new people into your children's lives is something that will happen naturally over time and should not be rushed. Your happiness is important but your children's security and feelings are important too and should not be ignored or considered to be any less important.

It really is a good idea not to rush into things. Children can become attached to new people very quickly and form emotional relationships that are then left in tatters if the relationship doesn't work out. Consider your own situation and look at why your children are now part of a single-parent family. The reason for them being with just one parent will have a lot of bearing on how they respond to new people and how quickly they form an attachment. Some children will cling desperately to a potential new 'parent' to try and fill an emotional gap in their lives. Losing this new person can have devastating consequences for them.

Real life stories

'When is the right time? I didn't have a boyfriend for a very long time after my husband left and my children were very young, just babies really. I really liked this guy but kept him at arm's length for ages because I was so worried about the children getting too close to him. He really wanted to get to know them quickly, but I had so many worries! He was a dad already and knew all about children, but I was still worried!' Jo, 35, single mum to two boys.

'It took a while before I had the confidence to introduce my new girlfriend to the children. When I did, it was a bit of a disaster to start with because she overindulged them - almost as if she was trying too hard and wanted to buy their affections. I had to talk to her about it and she got very upset, but it all worked out in the end. We just needed to find our way through the change in all our lives.' Ben, 40, single dad to two girls.

'Things are a bit different from when we were teenagers and our eyes met across a smoky disco! These days we have children, ex partners, jobs, mortgages and all the other baggage that comes with having had a life already - going out there to try and find someone prepared to take all that on was never going to be easy!'

Sue, 42, single mum to three children, works full time.

What you need to remember

- Having a life of your own and a new relationship is allowed, so you shouldn't feel guilty!

- Consider your children's needs ahead of your own though and make sure you think carefully before you introduce the idea of a new partner.

- Relate offer great advice for people in your situation and have a website and books to help you.

- Everyone will give you different advice, but unless they have been through the same situation as you, they really won't understand what you are going through. However, remember that your true friends only have your best interests at heart and want to help you make the right decisions.

- Life has a habit of falling naturally into place; there is no time limit and everyone's situation will be different. If it doesn't feel like the right time to introduce your children to someone new, then wait. If your new partner really wants to have a proper relationship with you, they won't mind waiting.

Moving on

When and if you do meet your new Mr or Miss Right, there will be lots of practical issues that need to be addressed. Initially you will be excited and nervous about dating again and going through all the getting to know each other stages.

Once you start to settle in to your new relationship and your children have got used to the idea that you have a new partner, you will find that your life may start to change and develop in different ways and you will need to think about finding ways of managing your changing circumstances.

There is a wealth of professional advice and support available to help you navigate your way through the process of blending families and relationships. However, many people discover that as time goes on they find their own ways of dealing with things.

'When we took the step to move in together we had to sell both of our houses and then put all the money together to buy one big house for us and the four children. It was a major step and I knew it would be difficult but it has all worked out. Nobody can really prepare you for a big change like that, but as long as you communicate with each other and are honest and open about your worries then it will be okay.' Jane, 44.

- Take things at your own pace - don't be pressured into rushing into making decisions just because other people think you should or shouldn't do something.

- Things can change. You might make a decision one day and then change your mind the next. This is normal and all part of the process.

- Trusting new people in your life takes time. Give yourself time to adjust and settle in to a new relationship. Don't rush and don't write the script - nobody really knows what will happen next.

- Remember to have fun! There really aren't any hard and fast rules and you have to learn to recognise if you are uncomfortable with a situation and find a way of coping with it.

- Moving on can be hard but it is all part of life. Take your time and do things when you and your children are ready.

Summing Up

Dating again can be fraught with worry because it means stepping outside of your comfort zone and facing things that are a bit scary and different.

Getting your confidence back after the breakdown of a relationship is never easy, and you may feel that your only identity is that of parent. It's hard to imagine being with someone else and you may even feel that you don't have much to say about your life that anyone else will find interesting.

Be assured that this is not the case at all! If you are lacking in confidence and have a few single friends, why not organise a night out together? Who knows, you may even bump into another group of singles!

Starting your life again with a young family in tow is hard work, stressful and difficult at times, but you can do it and you will.

Chapter Nine

So, What Next?

By the time you have reached this final chapter of the book, you should be well on the way to creating a new life for you and your children as a single parent.

All the initial emotional pressures should be starting to ease off and you should be settling in to your new role. There may well still be legal and financial issues hanging over you, and from experience these may well take several years to resolve. However, it is still important to keep moving forward and think positively about your situation.

Ensuring that your children are happy, settled and secure with their lives is the most important thing you can do, as well as taking care of your own emotional health and wellbeing. This is a great time for planning your family's future and making decisions about your career, your home and what you want to do next.

You may feel completely content to be single and have no desire to meet another partner, preferring to put all your efforts into your family and work at this stage in your life. That's fine, provided that you do have time for yourself and a life outside of the home environment. Remember that one day your children will leave home and then your role as parent will be very different.

You may be at the stage where you feel it is time for a house move or even a move to another country. If you have always wanted to go and live in a farmhouse in France, and you have the ability to make this happen, now could be the time to start making plans.

Some quotes from some inspirational single parents

'For as long as I can remember, I have wanted to live in France and be an artist. I love art and painting but while I was bringing up my four boys as a single parent I didn't have the chance to do this. My youngest child is 18 and studying music at college and my eldest is 27, so I finally feel that I can let go and get on with my life! There is light after the tunnel!' Lesley, 47.

'Early in your life as a single parent you will find that the smallest tasks seem unachievable, but this is not because you can't do them, it's because your situation is stressful, hard work and completely exhausting. I wanted to do so many things and got so frustrated because everyone seemed to be doing things quicker and better than I could. It was because they had the support of a partner. I was doing it all on my own.' Jan, 44.

'I made the mistake of not asking for help and pretending that I could afford to carry on living the lifestyle that I had always had. Times have been tough financially but I am coming out of the other side now. It's still not easy and I will never be a millionaire, but life is good and I am happy. I have embraced being a single parent and I am proud of what I have done.' Anon.

'I still can't always believe that I have my own home. My ex husband tried to make things so hard for me, but I am not bitter because I feel I have really done a lot with my life and done the best I can for my children. We are a happy family and I have a great career and social life. There is life after being a single parent and I am proof of that!' Sarah, 40.

Make a plan

Where do you want to be in three years, five years, 10 years time? We are all allowed to have plans and dreams, ideas and ambitions - even single parents! Get a notebook and write a list of things in your life that are great and things that need attention. Perhaps you want to have paid off all your debts in three years? If you want to do this, how are you going to make it happen? Maybe you want to start your own business and with all the children off to school you can finally get this off the ground.

Everything takes time; be patient and don't feel under pressure to do things that other people are doing. Chances are that they have lots of help and support, two incomes and a fraction of the worries that you have on your own. So what if it takes you five years to earn enough money to get a mortgage - you will have done it on your own and that is a huge achievement.

I hope this book has proved to be a useful guide and has given you some ideas, advice and inspiration to help you create a life for you and your family.

Good luck!

Help List

Parenting, family help and support

Care for the Family

Garth House, Leon Avenue, Cardiff, CF15 7RG
Tel: 029 2081 0800
mail@cff.org.uk
www.careforthefamily.org.uk
This is a national charity which aims to promote strong family life and to help those affected by family breakdown. They do this through events, resources, training and networks of befrienders. Visit the website to sign up to their free monthly email newsletter.

Dad Info

www.dad.info
Dad Info provides information on a wide range of issues - from relationships and money to workplace rights and coping with separation. You can enter competitions, purchase publications and read relevant articles. Email your queries through the website.

Family Mediators Association

Tel: 0800 200 0033 (helpline – freephone)
www.thefma.co.uk
Family mediation is a voluntary process by which couples in dispute, particularly those going through separation or divorce, are helped to deal with arrangements for their future. The Family Mediators Association provides advice for couples considering separation or divorce and can put you in touch with a mediator. Free factsheets are provided on the website.

Family Rapp

Tel: 01883 723710
info@familyrapp.com
www.familyrapp.com
This is an online magazine for parents and carers of children between the ages of three and 13. The website contains a database of articles and links to cover both younger and older children.

Family Welfare Association (FWA)

501-505 Kingsland Road, London, E8 4AU
Tel: 0207 254 6251 (Monday and Friday only)
www.fwa.org.uk
FWA is the UK's leading family charity, supporting over 45,000 families every year. They tackle some of the most complex and difficult issues facing families today - including domestic abuse, mental health problems, learning disabilities and severe financial hardship.

For Parents by Parents

www.forparentsbyparents.com
Created in 2001 by two parents who wanted to provide a website for other parents, this site continues to be run by parents who believe that collectively parents are the best source of support to each other. This site provides advice, personal experiences and information on everything from finance and legal issues to work and personal issues. Well worth a visit!

Freecycle Network

http://uk.freecycle.org
This network is made up of many individual groups across the globe. It's a grassroots movement of people who are giving (and getting) stuff for free in their own towns. Visit the website to find your local group.

Gingerbread

Tel: 0800 018 5026 (lone parent helpline)
info@oneparentfamilies.org.uk
www.gingerbread.org.uk

www.oneparentfamilies.org.uk
Gingerbread has merged with One Parent Families to provide better support and a bigger voice to 1.8 million lone parents and their children in England and Wales. Visit the website for free factsheets, information and advice.

Home Dad

www.homedad.org.uk
Whatever your situation, Home Dad UK is dedicated to helping dads at home with their kids. Run by a team of stay at home dads, membership is free. Visit their website for information and advice.

Lone Parents

Freepost RLZJ-UBJX-TARZ, Lone Parents.org, Penrith, Cumbria, CA10 3SU
www.loneparents.org
The site offers help and support to lone parents who are finding it difficult to cope alone. Lone parents can find a safe place to meet other lone parents and chat to friends online, or to find some mutual support from others in the same situation.

One Parent Family

www.oneparentfamily.co.uk
This is an online club for single parents. Single parents can contact each other with all kinds of problems and queries, asking for advice and support from others who have already experienced a similar situation in their past.

Parentline Plus

520 Highgate Studios, 53-79 Highgate Road, Kentish Town, London, NW5 1TL
Tel: 0808 800 2222 (helpline)
www.parentlineplus.org.uk
Parentline Plus is for parents and carers and is a national charity that works for, and with, parents. Parentline Plus works to offer help and support through an innovative range of free, flexible, responsive services - shaped by parents for parents.

Raising Kids

Tel: 0208 444 4852 (general enquiries)
www.raisingkids.co.uk

This site offers support, information and friendship to everyone who's raising kids - whatever your circumstances or income. Join the online discussions or speak to an expert for advice. Finance, nutrition, education – it's all covered!

Relate

Tel: 0300 100 1234 (to find your local centre)
www.relate.org.uk
Relate is for people who want to make their family relationships better. They help people make sense of what's happening in their relationships, decide what they want to do and make those changes. Relate works with couples, individuals and families through a national network of Relate Centres and via email and phone counselling. Visit the website for a list of centres.

Single Mum Survival Guide

www.singlemumsurvivalguide.co.uk
Packed with practical information, this online survival guide offers support and forums where you can share your concerns with other single mums and swap advice and tips. Information is provided on issues including dating, finance, the best shopping deals and careers.

Single Parents Action Network (SPAN)

SPAN, Millpond, Baptist Street, Easton, Bristol, BS5 OXW
Tel: 0117 9514231
info@spanuk.org.uk
www.singleparents.org.uk
Online support from experienced single parents with real stories to tell. Their website provides news, views and information on all aspects of single parenting. Visit their new site for single parents at www.onespace.org.uk.

Single Parent Fun

www.singleparentfun.com
Singleparentfun.com is about bringing single parents together to share experiences and have fun. Make new friends, chat, organise days out and enjoy group holidays with other single parents. All can be arranged through your own personal account page.

Single Parents on Holiday

Unit 3, 4 Page Heath Lane, Bromley, BR1 2DS
Tel: 0871 550 4053
info@singleparentsonholiday.co.uk
www.singleparentsonholiday.co.uk
Single Parents on Holiday was founded to meet the needs of single parent families. Frustrated with the lack of holidays on offer that met the desires of single parents and their children, they designed a range of quality yet affordable single parent holidays. Checkout their beach, activity and skiing holidays.

Single Parents UK

www.singleparents.org.uk
An online community for single parents with discussions, information and advice.

One Space

www.onespace.org.uk
Find information and ideas to help you, or join online groups to share the load with other lone parents.

One Up Magazine

Tel: 01787 223557
www.oneupmagazine.co.uk
The online magazine for single parents and step parents.

Youth Information

Eastgate House, 19-23 Humberstone Road, Leicester, LE5 3GJ
Tel: 0116 242 7350
www.youthinformation.com
Youthinformation.com is The National Youth Agency's online information toolkit for young people and all those working with them. The website is packed with information on a range of issues, including divided families and divorce and separation.

Working and childcare

Childcare Link

Opportunity Links, Trust Court, Vision Park, Histon, Cambridge, CB4 9PW
childcarelink@opp-links.org.uk
www.childcarelink.gov.uk
Childcare Link provides details of local childcare providers in England as well
as general information about childcare. The site provides details of your local
Children's Information Services who provide advice on all aspects of childcare
and can put you in touch with registered childminders and nurseries.

Daycare Trust

Daycare Trust, 21 St George's Road, London, SE1 6ES
Tel: 020 7840 3350 (helpline Mondays, Wednesdays and Fridays 10.00am
- 5.00pm)
info@daycaretrust.org.uk
www.daycaretrust.org.uk
The Daycare Trust provides free information on a range of childcare issues
including childcare options, where to find childcare and how to find help with
childcare costs.

Net Mums

124, Mildred Avenue, Watford, WD18 7DX
www.netmums.com
Net Mums is a local network for mums and dads, offering a wealth of
information on both a national and local level. Once you have registered on
your local site you can access details for local resources, places to go and
chat with other parents online.

Legal support

Citizens Advice Bureau

www.citizensadvice.org.uk

The Citizens Advice Bureau provides up-to-date independent advice on issues covering a wide range of topics including benefits and housing, employment rights and discrimination, debt and tax issues. Visit the website for information, factsheets and contact details of your local office.

Divorce Online

www.divorce-online.co.uk
Provides information and advice on divorce. News, forums and finance calculators are included on the website.

Resolution (The Family Law Association)

Central Office, PO Box 302, Orpington, Kent, BR6 8QX
Tel: 01689 820272
info@resolution.org.uk
www.resolution.org.uk
This website gives you contact names, addresses and telephone numbers for solicitors who are trying to take the confrontation out of family law proceedings. Also offered are factsheets on issues such as divorce, mediation and children's rights, and a page with information on parenting after parting.

Counselling and therapy

British Association for Counselling & Psychotherapy (BACP)

BACP House, 15 St John's Business Park, Lutterworth, Leicestershire, LE17 4HB
www.bacp.co.uk
Tel: 01455 883300 (general enquiries)
bacp@bacp.co.uk
This is the main body for accreditation of counsellors. The site puts you in touch with therapists in your area.

Cruse Bereavement Care

Tel: 0844 477 9400 (helpline Monday to Friday 9.30am - 5pm)
helpline@cruse.org.uk

www.cruse.org.uk
Cruse Bereavement exists to promote the well-being of bereaved people and to enable anyone bereaved by death to understand their grief and cope with their loss. The organisation provides support and offers information, advice, education and training services.

Financial and housing advice

Askbaby.com

Askbaby.com, 2nd Floor, 16 Borough High Street, London, SE1 9QG
www.askbaby.com
Packed with information, this website is not only a guide to pregnancy and babycare, but looks at the range of benefits and financial help available.

Child Benefit

Tel: 0845 302 1444
Northern Ireland: 0845 603 2000
www.inlandrevenue.gov.uk/childbenefit/
Visit the website for information on child benefit; what it is and how to claim. Free leaflets are available to download.

Directgov

www.direct.gov.uk
This government website explains what is available in terms of credits and benefits.

Entitled To

www.entitledto.co.uk
This website has calculators and information to help you work out what you are entitled to.

Job Centre Plus

www.jobcentreplus.gov.uk
Provides information on benefits and claims, and what you are entitled to.

National Debtline

Tel: 0808 808 4000
www.nationaldebtline.co.uk
This helpline provides free, confidential and independent advice on how to deal with debt problems.

Shelter

Tel: 0808 800 4444 (free housing advice helpline)
www.shelter.org.uk
Shelter provides information and help with housing issues.

uSwitch

uSwitch Ltd, 111 Buckingham Palace Road, London, SW1W 0SR
Tel: 0800 404 7908
CustomerServices@uswitch.com
www.uswitch.com/debtadvicecentre/Single-Parents.html
uSwitch offer debt advice for single parents.

Working Tax Credit/Child Tax Credit Helpline

Tel: 0845 300 39000 (open 8am - 8pm, Monday to Friday)

Dating websites

Dating for Parents

www.datingforparents.com

Kids No Object

www.kno.org.uk

Lone Parents

www.lone-parents.org.uk/dating.htm

Parents Already

www.parentsalready.com

Other Single Parents

www.othersingleparents.com

Book List

Divorce and Separation – The Essential Guide
By Linda Jones, Need2Know, Peterborough, 2008, £8.99.

Help Children Cope With Divorce
By Paula Hall, Relate, UK, 2007, £8.99.

How to Succeed as a Single Parent
By Diane Louise Jordan, Maher Books, 2008, £3.50.

Single Mother's Survival Guide
By Patrick Karst, Woodys UK, 2000, £23.99.

Single Parenting for Dummies
By Marion Peterson, Dummies Guides, Wiley Publishing, Inc., UK, 2003, £13.95.

Your Money Or Your Life
By Alvin Hall, Coronet Books, USA, 2003, £7.99.